HOW TO DELETE BOOKS FROM KINDLE

A Step by Step Instruction Manual
on How to Delete Books on All Your
Kindle Devices In 2 Minutes

By

ADAMS BOSS

COPYRIGHT

TABLE OF CONTENT

CHAPTER 1

INTRODUCTION

Sometimes there are a lot of books they we have read and are occupying space on our kindle device and we find it difficult to uninstall this books on our kindle device You will learn how to uninstall this apps on all your Kindle device

*Kindle Keyboard

*Kindle Paper white

*Kindle Voyage

*Kindle Fire

*Kindle app for Android and ios

*Kindle Cloud

CHAPTER 2

HOW TO DELETE BOOKS ON A KINDLE PAPERWHITE IN 2 MINUTES

In order to remove books from your kindle paper white device

*Start by pressing and holding the book cover on the home screen

*When the dialog box displays, click on Remove from Device

The book will be deleted from your device but will be stored in cloud in case you want to download it

CHAPTER 3

HOW TO DELETE BOOKS ON A KINDLE VOYAGE IN 2 MINUTES

In order to remove books from Kindle voyage,

*Start by pressing and holding the book you want to remove for about 5 seconds and an option will display

*Next select "Remove from Device" and the book will be deleted automatically from kindle voyage

But you can read this book anytime by downloading it from Kindle Cloud again

CHAPTER 4

HOW TO DELETE BOOKS ON A KINDLE FIRE HD IN 2 MINUTES

In order to delete books from Kindle Fire

*Start by pressing and holding the book to show the menu and select Remove from Device

The book will be deleted from your Fire HD but will be available on Cloud in case you want it again

CHAPTER 5

HOW TO DELETE BOOKS ON A KINDLE APP ON ANDROID AND IOS IN 2 MINUTES

ON KINDLE ANDROID APP

In order to remove books from your kindle app installed on your Android device,

*Start by clicking on the application

*Next go to the home screen and display your books

*Next search for the book you want to remove from your phone in the kindle app, press and hold the book you want to delete and then select "Remove from device"

ON KINDLE IOS APP

This allows you to delete books on iPad, iPhone

To remove books on your device

*Start by clicking on the cover of the book you want to delete and hold the cover of the book and then click on "Remove from device"

CHAPTER 6

HOW TO SUCCESSFULLY DELETE BOOKS ON KINDLE CLOUD IN 2 MINUTES

Kindle cloud is where all the books that you have purchased and downloaded free can be stored, once you delete books from kindle cloud you will not be able to read the books until you have downloaded it again or buy it

To do this

*Start by going to www.amazon.com

*Login to your Amazon.com and got to "Manage your Content and Devices"

When this appears, all the items in your Kindle Cloud will appear

*Next select the books you want to delete, and click on "Delete Button"

*Next a Window will appear warning you Click "Yes" to continue

*You have deleted the book permanently from your device

THE END

Adams Boss

Adams Boss

Adams Boss

Adams Boss

Adams Boss

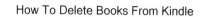

Adams Boss